RETURNING TO
THE PIANO
A REFRESHER BOOK FOR ADULTS

BY WENDY STEVENS

Perhaps you are one of the many individuals who has said, "I wish I hadn't stopped playing the piano!" No matter what age, the desire to create music for ourselves and others to enjoy never leaves us. But as busy adults, we want to play the music we *know and love*. If you are one of these individuals, *Returning to the Piano* is the book for you. In this book, you will find popular songs, folk songs, and familiar classical music that will inspire you and keep you motivated.

This book is especially tailored to a student who is returning to the piano after taking several years of lessons as a child. Each of the six units in this book discusses concepts you have been exposed to in these years of music study but may need to review as an adult.

The CD that accompanies this book will help you learn pieces more quickly, play them more musically, and bring more enjoyment to your practice time. The first track contains the piano solo with accompaniment at a slower tempo and the second track contains the accompaniment at a slightly faster tempo. Answers to theory exercises can be found in the back of this book.

I hope that you will enjoy the variety of popular, classical, and folk tunes in this book as you embark on your exciting quest to return to the piano!

Happy Music Making!

Wendy Stevens

Acknowledgements

I'd like to thank my editor, Jennifer Linn, for her confidence in me and excitement for this project. Her keen eye for detail and appealing ideas have made this book a fun and rewarding adventure.

I'd like to thank the following pedagogues for their incredible influence in my musical life: Dr. Sylvia Coats for her support and influence in piano pedagogy, Dr. Walter Mays for his friendship, inspiration, and instruction on composing, Paul Reed for teaching me to listen, and Elaina Owens Duncan, my childhood piano teacher. I especially thank my husband, Richard Stevens, for encouraging me to find and appreciate good elements in all genres of music.

ISBN 978-1-4234-6817-2

HAL•LEONARD®
CORPORATION

7777 W. BLUEMOUND RD. P.O. BOX 13819 MILWAUKEE, WI 53213

Visit Hal Leonard Online at
www.halleonard.com

Table of Contents

Review

Unit 1

Unit 2

Unit 3

Unit 4

Unit 5

Unit 6

Answer Key

Review of Music Terms and Symbols

Below is a list of music terms and symbols used in this book.

Terms

A tempo	Return to the original tempo
Accelerando (accel.)	Gradually speed up the tempo
Adagio	Slowly
Allegro	Quickly
Andante	Moderate, walking speed
Cantabile	In a singing style
Crescendo (cresc.)	Gradually get louder
Con fuoco	With fire
D.C. al Fine	*Da Capo al Fine* (pronounced fee-náy). Repeat from the beginning until the word *Fine*.
D.S. al Coda	*Dal Segno al Coda*. Repeat from the *Segno* sign until the *Coda* sign. At the *Coda* sign, jump to the *Coda*.
Diminuendo (dim.)	Gradually get softer
Interval	The difference in pitch between two notes
Legato	Play smoothly connected
Loco	Notes are played as written
Moderato	Moderately

Molto	Much	
Poco	A little	
Ritardando (rit.)	Gradually slow down the tempo	
Rubato	Literally means "stolen time." Used to indicate that the music is to be played freely with some variation in tempo.	
Simile	Continue in a similar manner	
Staccato	Play with a detached touch	
Subito (sub.)	Suddenly	

Dynamics

pp *Pianissimo*	Very soft	
p *Piano*	Soft	
mp *Mezzo Piano*	Medium soft	
mf *Mezzo Forte*	Medium loud	
f *Forte*	Loud	
ff *Fortissimo*	Very loud	
Crescendo	Gradually get louder	
Diminuendo	Gradually get softer	

Music Symbols

♭	**Flat sign**	Play the note a half step lower than written
♯	**Sharp sign**	Play the note a half step higher than written
♮	**Natural sign**	Play the note as written (the natural sign cancels a sharp or flat)
>	**Accent**	Play with more emphasis
𝄐	*Fermata*	Hold the note longer than the value indicated
	Tenuto	Hold the note for its full value
	Staccato	Play with a detached touch
	Tie	Hold the note for the combined value
	Slur	Play smoothly (see *legato*)
8va---	**8va sign**	Play the notes under the dotted line one octave higher
⊕	*Coda* **sign**	Used to indicate the place in which you move to the *Coda* in a *D.C. al Coda*
𝄋	*Dal Segno* **sign**	Used to indicate the place you repeat from in a *D.S. al Coda*

Note Names

Learning the Landmark notes will make it easier to read other notes on the staff.

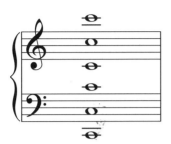

High C – 2 ledger lines from top
Treble C – 2 spaces from top

Middle C

Bass C – 2 spaces from bottom
Low C – 2 ledger lines from bottom

Treble G
Treble Clef = G clef
Wraps around G line

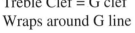

Bass F
Bass Clef = F clef
Sits on F line

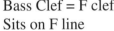

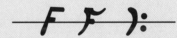

Early forms of the G (treble) clef

Early forms of the F (bass) clef

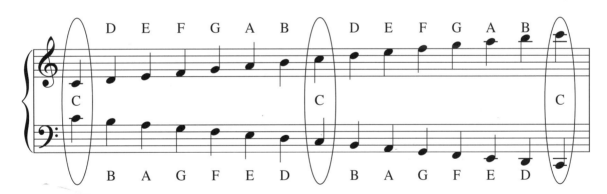

 Name these notes:

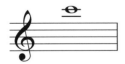

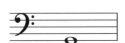

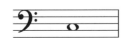

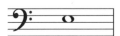

Answers on page 96

Intervals

An **interval** is the difference in pitch between two notes.

Melodic Interval: Notes are played separately  *Melodic 2nd*

Harmonic Interval: Notes are played together  *Harmonic 2nd*

2nd   3rd   4th   5th   6th   7th   8th (octave)

2nds, 4ths, 6ths, and **8ths** are written from a space to a line OR a line to a space.

3rds, 5ths and **7ths** are written from a space to a space OR a line to a line.

2nd   4th   6th   8th

3rd   5th   7th

2nd   4th   6th   8th

3rd   5th   7th

 Write the name of each interval in the blanks below.

_____ _____ _____ _____ _____ _____

_____ _____ _____ _____ _____ _____

Answers on page 96

Rhythm

The time signature of the piece tells how many beats are in a measure and what kind of note receives 1 beat.

$\frac{4}{4}$ 4 beats in a measure
A quarter note = 1 beat

$\frac{2}{4}$ 2 beats in a measure
A quarter note = 1 beat

$\frac{3}{4}$ 3 beats in a measure
A quarter note = 1 beat

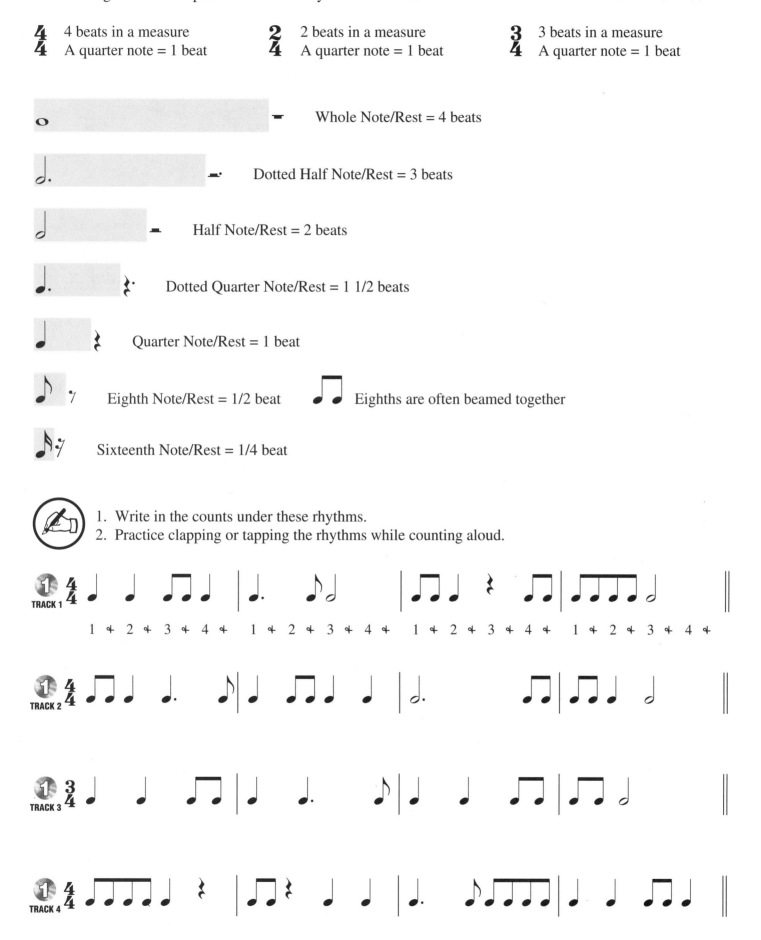

Whole Note/Rest = 4 beats

Dotted Half Note/Rest = 3 beats

Half Note/Rest = 2 beats

Dotted Quarter Note/Rest = 1 1/2 beats

Quarter Note/Rest = 1 beat

Eighth Note/Rest = 1/2 beat   Eighths are often beamed together

Sixteenth Note/Rest = 1/4 beat

1. Write in the counts under these rhythms.
2. Practice clapping or tapping the rhythms while counting aloud.

TRACK 1

1 + 2 + 3 + 4 +   1 + 2 + 3 + 4 +   1 + 2 + 3 + 4 +   1 + 2 + 3 + 4 +

TRACK 2

TRACK 3

TRACK 4

9

Technique

Practice these exercises every day to help your fingers become stronger and more coordinated.

Hanon Exercise No. 1

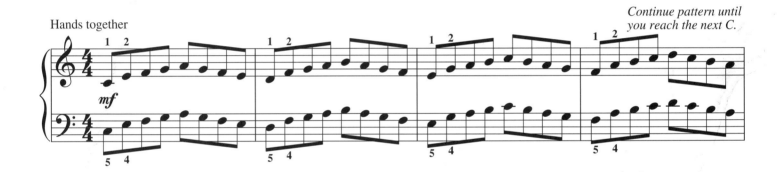

Practice strategies for busy adults:

- **Regular practice is best.** Five days of shorter practice segments are often better than one day of marathon practice.

- **Set small goals.** Break down your assignments into measurable goals. Give yourself small goals each day so that your progress can be measurable. Start with hands alone practice or work on just a few measures at a time.

- **Slow down.** If something seems difficult, one of the most helpful practice techniques is to slow down! Many problems can be solved by slowing down and giving your brain time to process all of the complicated tasks you are trying to do at once.

- **Ask questions.** You will make the most progress if you can become your own teacher. If you are having trouble with a section ask, "Why? Is it the speed, the fingering, the rhythm, the notes, the touch?" Focus on one element at a time rather than trying to solve all difficulties at once.

- **Don't expect too much too soon!** Everyone makes mistakes and no musician plays perfectly all of the time. It's OK to be human!

Unit 1

JESU, JOY OF MAN'S DESIRING

English Words by Robert Bridges
Music by Johann Sebastian Bach (1685–1750)
Arranged by Wendy Stevens

FORREST GUMP – MAIN TITLE

(Feather Theme)

from the Paramount Motion Picture FORREST GUMP

Music by Alan Silvestri
Arranged by Wendy Stevens

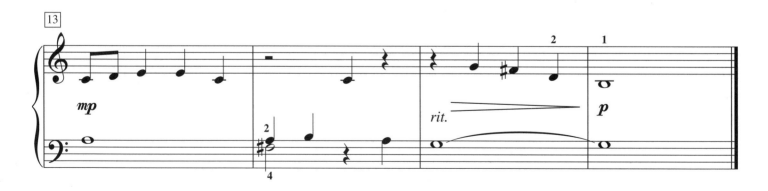

FANFARE

(Op. 117, No. 8)

By Cornelius Gurlitt (1820–1901)

TRACKS 9/10

Triumphantly (♩ = 132)

13

GAELIC MELODY

Traditional
Arranged by Wendy Stevens

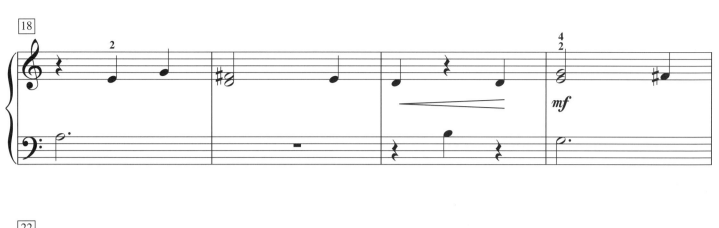

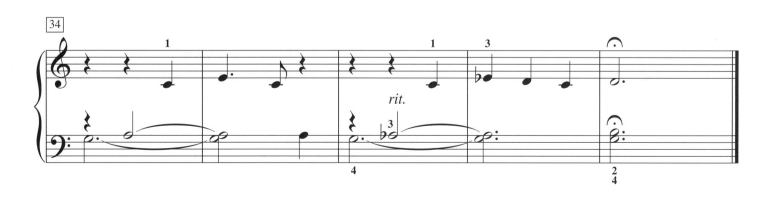

SIMPLE GIFTS

Traditional Shaker Hymn
Arranged by Wendy Stevens

ODE TO JOY

(from *Symphony No. 9*)

Words by Henry van Dyke
Music by Ludwig van Beethoven (1770–1827)
Arranged by Wendy Stevens

Unit 2

 Label the intervals in this piece.

> *8va* *8va* means to play one octave higher than written.

Hold the damper (right) pedal down throughout this piece.

SOLACE

By Wendy Stevens

Answers on page 96

Playing *Cantabile*

> *Cantabile* (pronounced kahn-tah-bi-lay) is Italian for "in a singing style." The *cantabile* melody should be more prominent than the accompaniment.

Playing a *cantabile* melody requires good balance between the hands. For good balance, the melody must be louder than the accompaniment. Use these practice steps to gain more control over the balance of the melody and accompaniment.

1. Practice the right hand alone, giving careful attention to the fingering.
2. "Ghost" the left hand (silently depress the notes) while the right hand plays.
3. Play both hands audibly, keeping the left hand softer than the right hand.

Pathetique Sonata Exercise

Left hand blocking

This exercise combines the eighth notes in the left hand of the original arrangement into more manageable partner note units. This is called "blocking" and is an effective practice strategy for learning pieces more quickly and for learning to balance the melody and accompaniment.

Now add the right hand, keeping the left hand softer than the melody. Practice this exercise using the three tips for playing *cantabile* listed above.

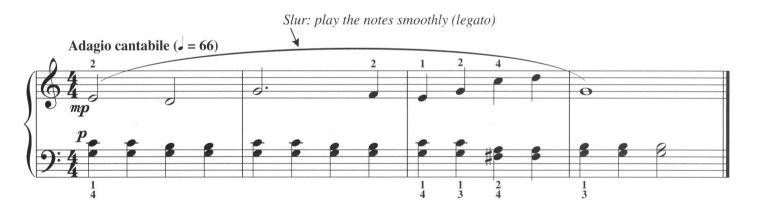

Slur: play the notes smoothly (legato)

19

PATHETIQUE SONATA

(2nd Movement Theme from *Sonata No. 8, Op. 13*)

By Ludwig van Beethoven (1770–1827)
Arranged by Wendy Stevens

TRACKS
19/20

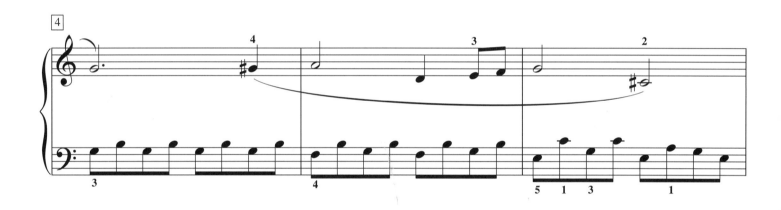

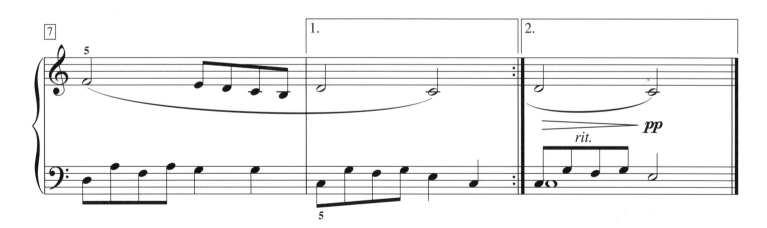

Scales

A scale is a pattern of whole and half steps. A major scale contains the following whole and half step pattern:

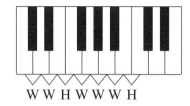

W W H W W W H

C Major Scale

Becoming fluid with the finger crossings in scales will help you play many similar scale passages in pieces. As you play the first three notes in the right hand, your thumb will pass *under* the 2nd and 3rd finger. When your thumb plays the F, it will play on its *side tip*.

After you play the first five notes of the left hand, the 3rd finger will cross *over* the 1st finger. As the scale descends, the thumb will pass under the 2nd and 3rd finger, again playing on its *side tip*.

Primary Chords in Root Position

Primary chords are built on the 1st, 4th, and 5th notes in a scale, thus the I, IV, V designation. The V7 chord adds an interval of a 7th above the root.

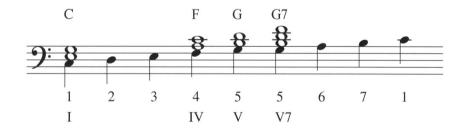

Letters are used in popular music to indicate the chords intended to harmonize a given melody.
Roman numerals are typically used in classical music to analyze the harmonic structure of a piece.
The Roman numeral indicates the root of the chord based on the key signature.

Chord Progression

Primary chords are easier when played in a chord progression, which rearranges the notes into inversions that are more accessible to the hands. The roots of these chords are designated in black.

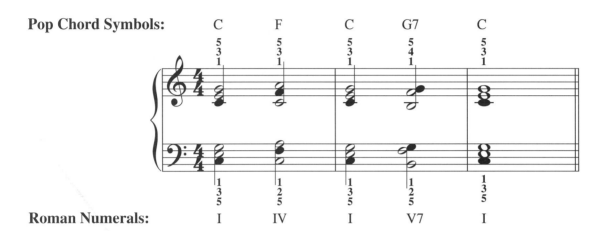

Arpeggio

An arpeggio is a broken chord in which the notes are played in sequence up or down.

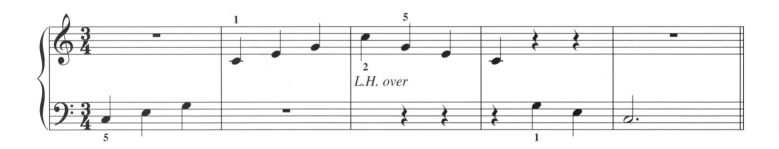

Lead Sheets

A lead sheet is a type of music in which only the melody is notated, often with lyrics and chord symbols. The performer is left to fill in the harmony based on the chord symbols indicated.

C Major Chord Progression

Use the chords from the C Major Chord Progression in the following tunes.

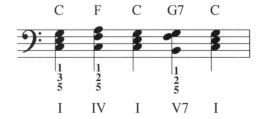

Alouette

1. Play the right-hand melody alone.
2. Play the melody with blocked chords in the left hand where indicated by the chord symbols.

For He's a Jolly Good Fellow

1. Play the right-hand melody alone.
2. Play the melody with blocked chords in the left hand where indicated by the chord symbols.

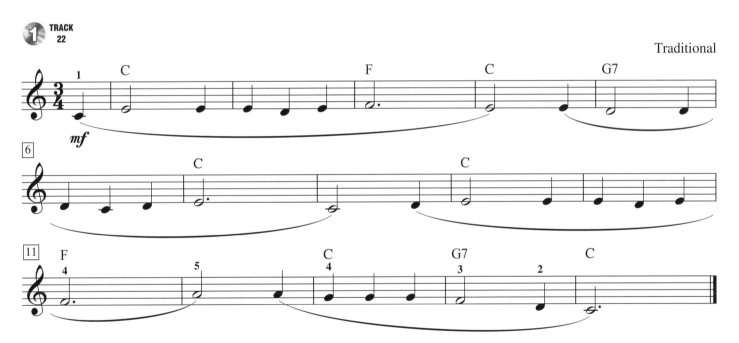

Practice this right-hand exercise to prepare for the scale passages in "Twinkle, Twinkle."

TWINKLE, TWINKLE
(In Classical Style)

Traditional
Arranged by Wendy Stevens

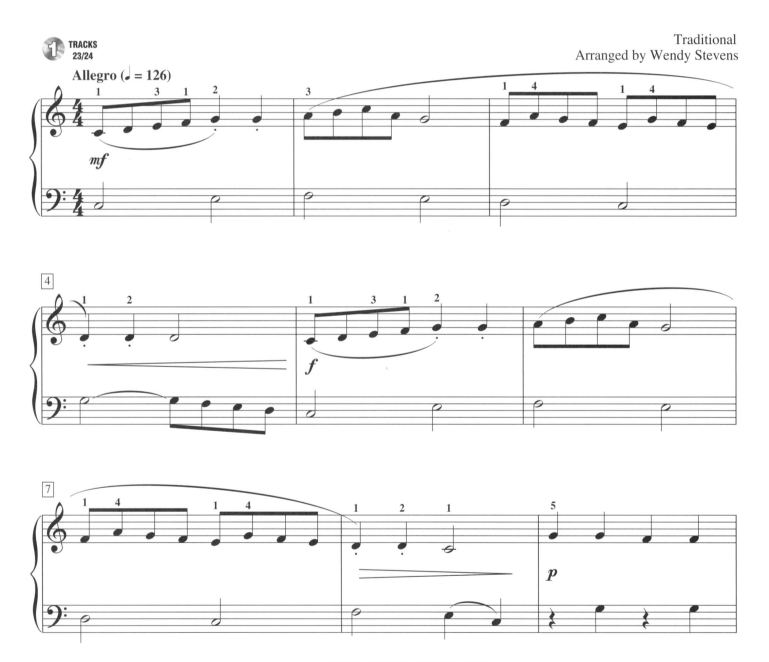

The Classical period of music history dates from 1750–1800. Mozart, Haydn and Beethoven were all composers who wrote in the Classical period. This style of music is characterized by clean and simple textures, much like the clean lines of architecture in Classical style buildings. Classical music often consists of one melody and an accompaniment. To give the Classical style the elegance and balance that it requires, careful attention should be given to ensure that the articulation (*staccato, legato,* accents) and note values are played with precision.

RONDEAU

(Theme from *Masterpiece Theatre*)

By Jean-Joseph Mouret (1682–1738)
Arranged by Wendy Stevens

Accompaniment (With duet, play solo one octave higher)

tenuto: hold for full value

G Major Scale

 Circle the Fs that are made sharp by the key signature.

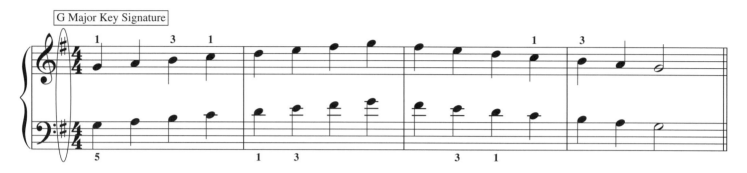

Primary Chords in Root Position

Primary chords are built on the 1st, 4th, and 5th notes in a scale, thus the I, IV, V designation. The V7 chord adds an interval of a 7th above the root.

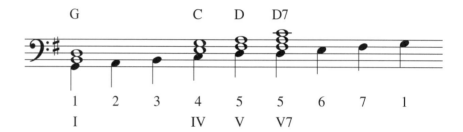

Chord Progression

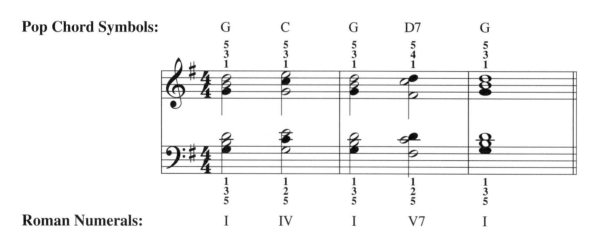

Arpeggio

28

Practice this left-hand exercise to prepare for the hand shifts in "Turkey in the Straw."

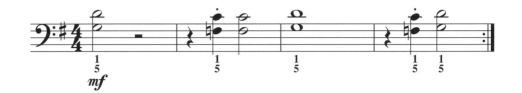

TURKEY IN THE STRAW

American Folksong
Arranged by Wendy Stevens

I WALK THE LINE

TRACKS
29/30

Words and Music by John R. Cash
Arranged by Wendy Stevens

Sauntering ($\text{♩} = 192$)

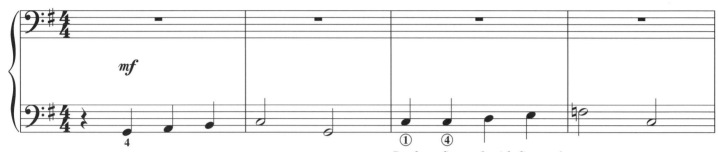

Replace finger 1 with finger 4

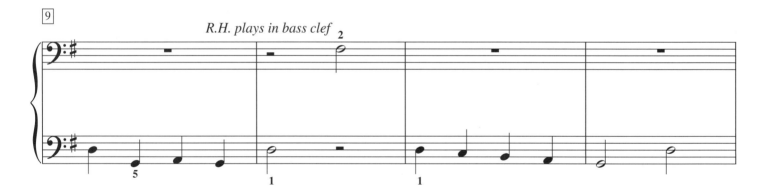

R.H. plays in bass clef

I keep a close watch on this heart of mine.

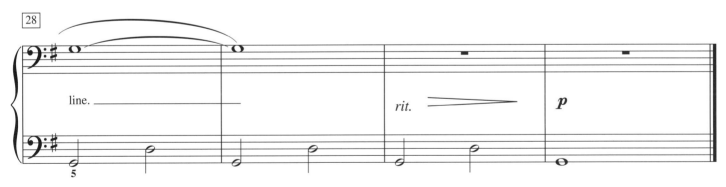

"I Walk the Line" was written by Johnny Cash and recorded in 1956. Johnny was particularly fond of the sound of the snare drum, but since he performed with so few musicians at the beginning of his career, this was not available to him. Instead, Johnny would often position a piece of paper in his guitar strings to create his own unique snare drum sound.

Syncopation

Syncopation occurs when notes land on normally un-accented beats. In $\frac{4}{4}$ meter, the natural accents occur on beats 1 and 3. Secondary accents occur on beats 2 and 4.

𝄾 An eighth rest gets a half beat.

1. Write in the counts under these rhythms from "Sweet Home Alabama."
2. Practice tapping the rhythms while counting aloud. The syncopation occurs in measure 4 where the right-hand eighth note is tied to the half note. This same syncopation occurs in measure 24 of "Sweet Home Alabama."

SWEET HOME ALABAMA

Words and Music by Ronnie Van Zant,
Ed King and Gary Rossington
Arranged by Wendy Stevens

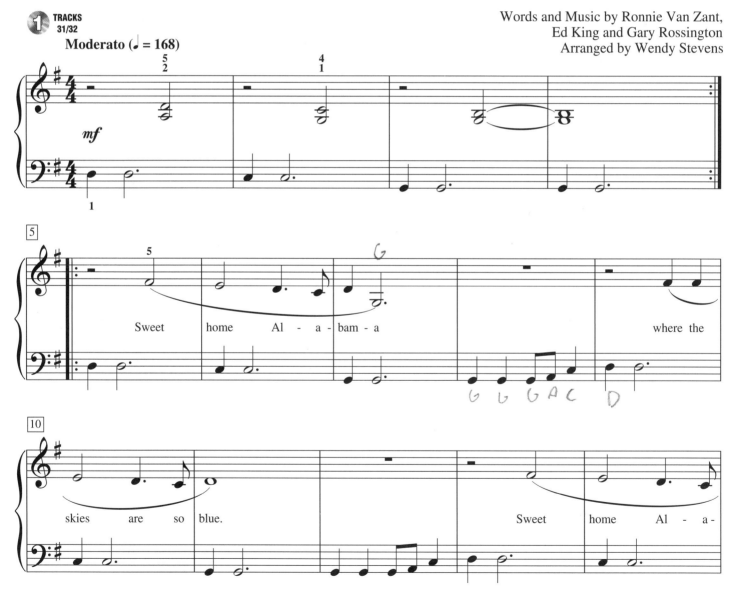

Can you find the syncopation that occurs in "Turkey in the Straw" (page 29)?

Answer on page 96

Unit 3

Pedal Technique

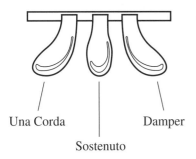

Una Corda

Sostenuto

Damper

Note: On some pianos, the middle pedal serves as a mute pedal. The pedal triggers a piece of felt to be placed between the hammer and strings, thereby muting the sound.

The **damper pedal** is used to sustain sounds and provide more resonance. To produce clear pedaling:

- Keep your right heel on the floor.
- *After* playing the notes, lift and immediately depress the pedal.
- Keep your foot in contact with the pedal at all times.

The **una corda pedal** ("soft pedal") is used to soften and change the color of the notes. The una corda pedal is played with the left foot. The **sostenuto pedal** sustains only the notes that are held as the pedal is depressed.

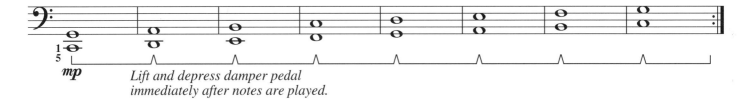

Lift and depress damper pedal immediately after notes are played.

SUMMER'S END

By Wendy Stevens

Leisurely ($\quad$ = 120)

Practice this exercise in preparation for "In Reflection."

IN REFLECTION

By Wendy Stevens

Practice this left-hand exercise to prepare for the hand shifts in "The Ash Grove." As soon as your left hand plays, begin moving to the new position. Your pedal will sustain the sounds.

THE ASH GROVE

Old Welsh Air
Arranged by Wendy Stevens

Many different sets of lyrics have been composed for this traditional Welsh tune. A popular set of lyrics was translated by John Oxenford in the 19th Century:

The ash grove how graceful, how plainly 'tis speaking,
The harp through it playing has language for me;
Whenever the light through its branches is breaking,
A host of kind faces is gazing on me.
The friends of my childhood again are before me,
Each step wakes a mem'ry as freely I roam,
With soft whispers laden the leaves rustle o'er me
The ash grove, the ash grove alone is my home.

ALLEGRO
(from *Eine kleine Nachtmusik*)

By Wolfgang Amadeus Mozart (1756–1791)
Arranged by Wendy Stevens

Mozart originally composed *Eine kleine Nachtmusik* for string quartet (2 violins, 1 viola, 1 cello),
though it is often performed by a string orchestra with multiple stringed instruments assigned to each part.
"Allegro" is the first of four movements.

1. Finish writing in the counts under the left-hand rhythms.
2. Practice tapping the rhythm while counting aloud to prepare for measures 17-20 of "Let It Be."

LET IT BE

Words and Music by John Lennon
and Paul McCartney
Arranged by Wendy Stevens

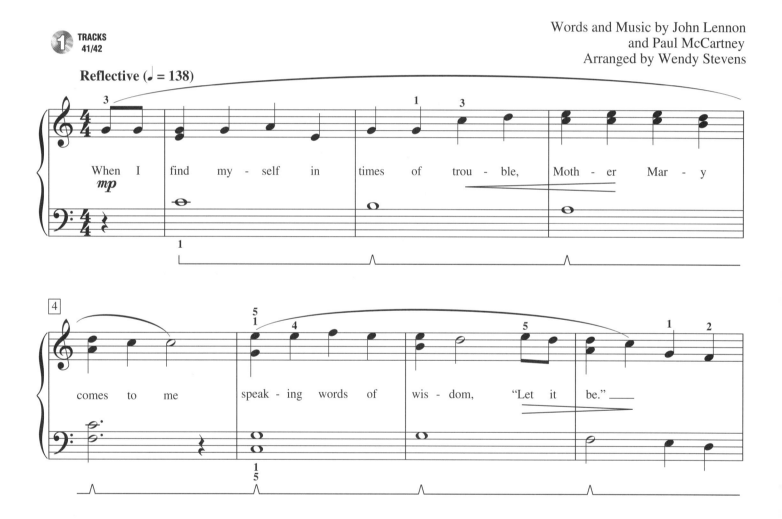

TO A WILD ROSE

(from *Woodland Sketches, Op. 51, No.1*)

By Edward MacDowell (1860–1908)
Arranged by Wendy Stevens

D.C. al Coda: *Da Capo al Coda* means to return to the beginning of the piece and play until the *coda* sign.
At the sign, jump to the *coda* and play to the end.

Coda sign: indicates the ending of the piece

POLOVTSIAN DANCE

(from *Prince Igor*)

By Alexander Borodin (1833–1887)
Arranged by Wendy Stevens

TRACKS
45/46

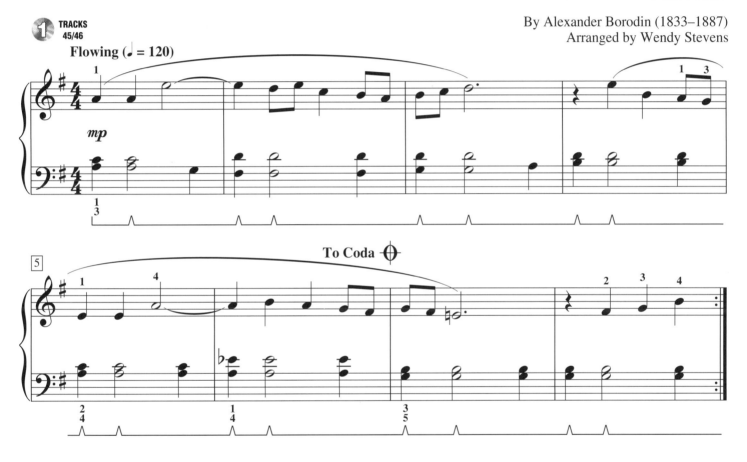

Accompaniment (With duet, play solo one octave higher)

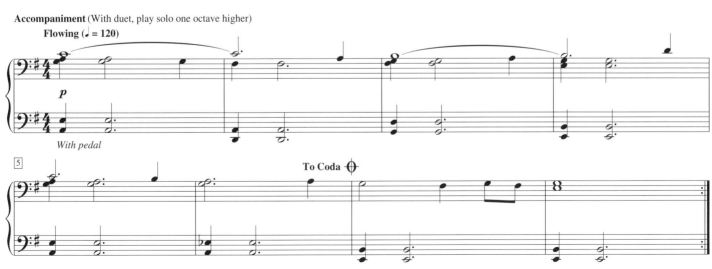

(Accompaniment)

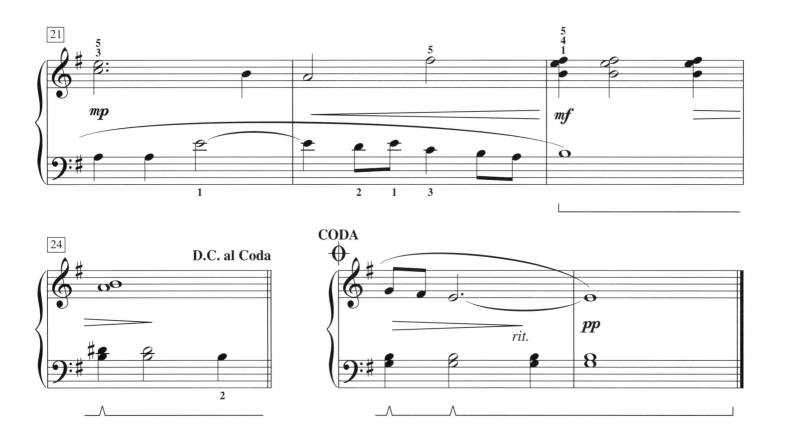

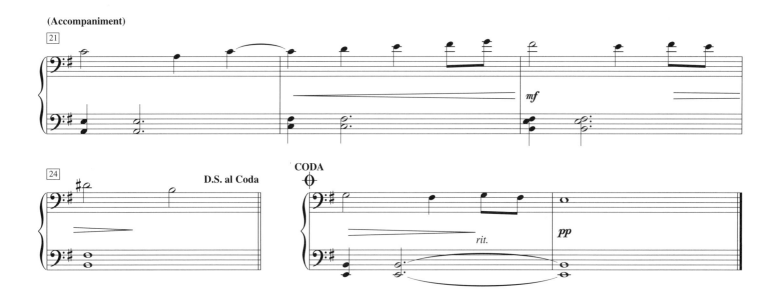

Alexander Borodin belonged to a group of Russian composers called *The Mighty Five* or *The Mighty Handful*. These nationalist composers were committed to writing a specifically Russian flavor of art music. Other composers in *The Mighty Handful* were Mily Balakirev (the leader), César Cui, Modest Mussorgsky, and Nikolai Rimsky-Korsakov.

Borodin made his living as a chemist, thus limiting the amount of music he composed. A number of his works were left unfinished upon his death, and were later completed by Rimsky-Korsakov and other Russian composers.

Twelve-Bar Blues

One of the most common styles of blues today is the twelve-bar blues. This twelve-bar chord progression uses a prescribed set and order of chords over which a musician can improvise a melody.

The **Chord Progression** for a twelve-bar blues piece is:

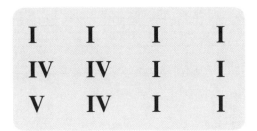

In the Key of C, the chords would be:

This five-finger blues scale can be played above the twelve-bar blues chord progression.

Swing It!

Jazz often requires the performer to "swing" the eighth notes. This is done by making the first eighth long and the second eighth short, resulting in a long-short pattern.

Long-short, long-short, long-short, long-short, long.

Improvising with the Twelve-Bar Blues

While listening to this accompaniment, improvise a melody using the five-finger blues scale.

By Wendy Stevens

TRACK 47

Swingin' (♩ = 116)

46

Practice this left-hand exercise to prepare for the chord changes in "Highway Blues."

HIGHWAY BLUES

This piece uses the traditional twelve-bar blues chord progression.

By Wendy Stevens

Practice this exercise to prepare for the fingering and rhythm of "Lean on Me."

LEAN ON ME

Words and Music by Bill Withers
Arranged by Wendy Stevens

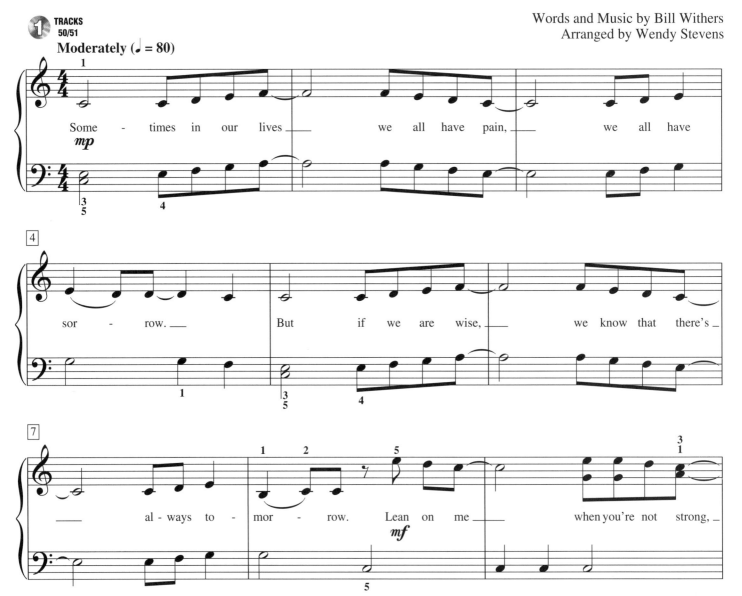

Some - times in our lives ___ we all have pain, ___ we all have

sor - row. ___ But if we are wise, ___ we know that there's ___

___ al - ways to - mor - row. Lean on me ___ when you're not strong, ___

Unit 4

Minor Scales

A minor scale has a different pattern of half steps and whole steps from the major scale and typically has a darker sound. This is the whole and half step pattern for the natural minor scale:

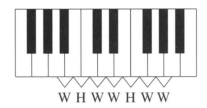

W H W W H W W

Every key signature can represent a major or a minor key. The ending notes or chord will usually indicate whether a piece is major or minor. The two keys are called "relative" because they share the same note names but begin on different notes. The relative minor scale can be constructed by playing the notes of the major scale but beginning on the 6th note of the major scale.

Finding the Relative Minor

To quickly find the "relative" minor of a Major Key Signature, count down 3 half steps.
For example,

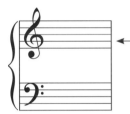

← **C Major Key Signature:**
Count down 3 half steps from C = **A Minor Key Signature**

A Minor ⟷ C Major
"Relative keys"

 Count down 3 half steps to find the relative Minor of these Major keys.

Major Key	Relative Minor
G Major	B-
F Major	D -
D Major	B-
C Major	A -

Use this keyboard to help
count the half steps.

Forms of the Minor Scale

There are three different types of minor scales:

The **natural minor** scale uses the same pitches as the relative major scale. The correct notes of the natural minor scale can be found by playing the same notes but starting on the 6th note of the major scale.

The **harmonic minor** scale raises the 7th note ascending and descending.

The **melodic minor** scale raises the 6th and 7th notes ascending and lowers them descending.

Answers on page 96

A Minor Scale

 What is A minor's relative major key?_____ (count up 3 half steps)

A Natural minor scale

The A natural minor scale has the same notes as C Major.

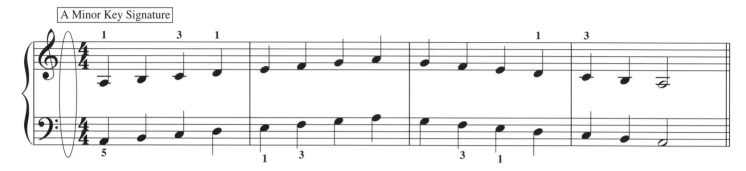

A Harmonic minor scale

Raise the 7th note ascending and descending.

A Melodic minor scale

Raise the 6th and 7th notes ascending and make them natural descending.

Primary Chords in Root Position

Primary chords are built on the 1st, 4th, and 5th notes in a scale, thus the i, iv, and V designation. The V7 chord adds an interval of a 7th above the root.

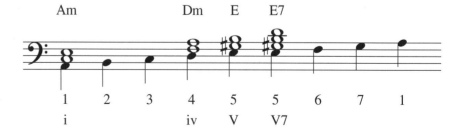

Theory Tip: Capital roman numerals indicate major chords (I, IV, V) while lower case roman numerals (i, iv) indicate minor chords. Pop chord symbols indicate major chords with capital letters (C, D, A) and minor chords with capital letters followed by a lower case "m" (Am, Dm, Cm).

Answers on page 96

Chord Progression

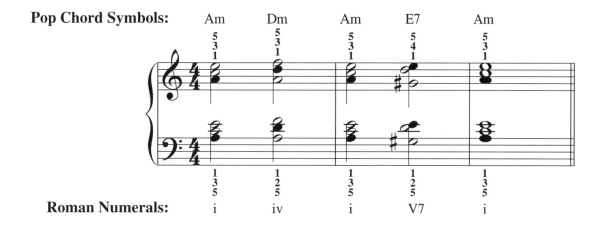

Arpeggio

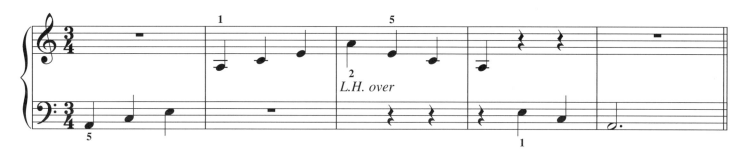

Playing from a Lead Sheet

Harmonizing in A minor

Joshua Fit the Battle of Jericho

1. Play the right-hand melody alone.
2. Play the melody with blocked chords in the left hand as indicated by the chord symbols.

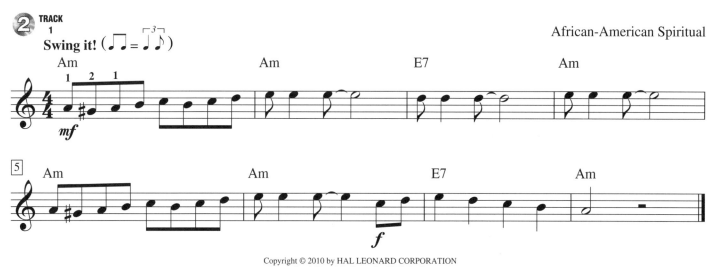

D.S. al Coda: *Dal Segno al Coda* means to return to the *Segno* sign and play until you see the *coda* sign, where you will then skip to the *coda*.

Segno **sign:** Return to this sign when you see *D.S. al Coda*.

WHERE DO I BEGIN

(Love Theme from the Paramount Picture LOVE STORY)

Words by Carl Sigman
Music by Francis Lai
Arranged by Wendy Stevens

14 heart. She fills my heart _____ with ver-y spe-cial things, _ with an-gels'

18 songs, _____ with wild i-mag-in-ings; _____ she fills my soul _____ with so much

21 love that an-y-where I go, _____ I'm nev-er lone-ly; _____ with her a-

24 round, _____ who could be lone-ly? _ I reach for her hand, _____ it's al-ways there. _____

28 *Go back to the sign at m. 3*
D.S. al Coda

CODA _____ and she'll be there. _____ *rit.* **_pp_**

D Minor Scale

 What is D minor's relative major key?_____ (count up 3 half steps)

Circle the Bs that are made flat by this key signature.
1. Play D Natural Minor Scale.
2. Play D Harmonic Minor Scale (raise the 7th note).

Primary Chords in Root Position

Primary chords are built on the 1st, 4th, and 5th notes in a scale, thus the i, iv, V designation. The V7 chord adds an interval of a 7th above the root.

Chord Progression

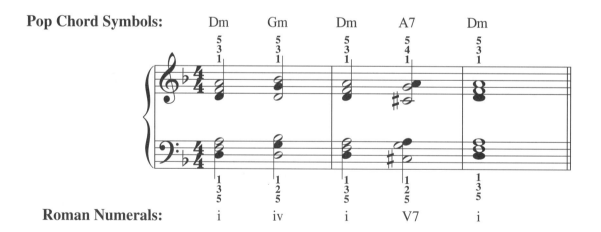

Arpeggio

Answers on page 96

IN THE HALL OF THE MOUNTAIN KING

(from *Peer Gynt, No. 1, Op. 46*)

By Edvard Grieg (1843–1907)
Arranged by Wendy Stevens

1. Listen to CD track 57 to help you feel the swing beat in "The Erie Canal."
2. Tap the following rhythm pattern from "The Erie Canal" while listening to the CD. Remember to swing the eighth notes.

THE ERIE CANAL

Traditional New York Work Song
Arranged by Wendy Stevens

E Minor Scale

 What is E minor's relative major key?_____ (count up 3 half steps)
Circle the Fs that are made sharp by this key signature.

1. Play E Natural Minor scale.
2. Play E Harmonic Minor scale (raise the 7th note).

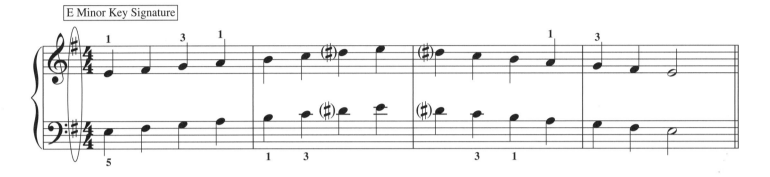

Primary Chords in Root Position

Primary chords are built on the 1st, 4th, and 5th notes in a scale, thus the i, iv, V designation. The V7 chord adds an interval of a 7th above the root.

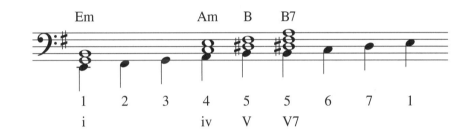

Chord Progression

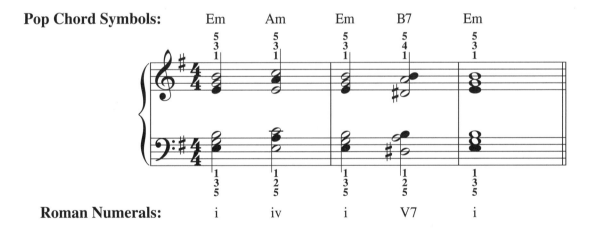

Arpeggio

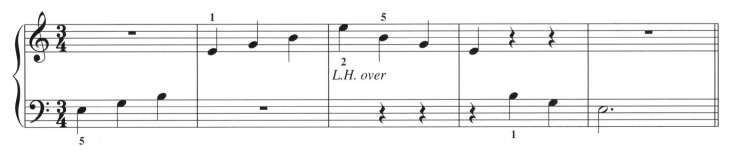

Answers on page 96

Expressive Playing

There are many ways to become more expressive in your playing. Some of the most basic ways include:

- Following dynamic markings
- Observing articulations (*staccato, legato,* accents)
- Observing tempo changes (*rit., a tempo, accel.,* etc.)

You can become even more expressive in your playing by following these principles:

1. When dynamic markings are not indicated, try a simple *crescendo* and *diminuendo* within the 4 or 8 measure phrase.

 Add a *crescendo* and *diminuendo* marking to the second line of "Scarborough Fair," then play the lead line with harmony added.

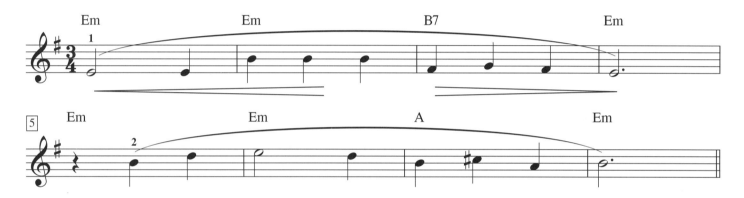

2. When dynamic markings are not indicated, often a *crescendo* to the highest note is appropriate.

 Add a *crescendo* marking and play this E minor arpeggio.

3. In some contexts it is appropriate to use *rubato*, which is Italian for "stolen time." The *rubato* marking indicates that the tempo is somewhat elastic, allowing the performer to speed up and slow down.

   To learn how to use *rubato* effectively, consider slowing slightly at the ends of phrases and moving ahead at the next phrase.

4. Make the dissonant passages or chords a little louder to pique interest and then "resolve" the dissonance by making the following consonant passage softer.

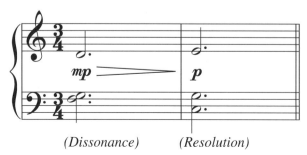

(Dissonance)   *(Resolution)*

Use *rubato* in this piece to be more expressive. Try slowing at the end of measures 7-8 and moving ahead in measures 9-10 as if pushing the momentum of the line forward. Add a *rit.* at an appropriate place on the last line.

Keep your right hand in the same relaxed shape while playing the 6ths.

LONGING FOR HOME

By Wendy Stevens

fp means to play *forte* on the first note, followed immediately by *piano*.

poco means "a little"

A **nocturne** ("Night Song") is a piece inspired by the night. Frederic Chopin is widely known for his twenty-one masterfully composed *Nocturnes*.

Use *rubato* freely in this expressive Nocturne.

NOCTURNE
(Op. 9, No. 2)

By Frederic Chopin (1810–1849)
Arranged by Wendy Stevens

Playing from Lead Sheets

Use the chords from the G Major chord progression to harmonize "Good Morning to All."

G Major Chord Progression

Good Morning to All

Words by Patty S. Hill
Music by Mildred J. Hill

Play R.H. one octave higher

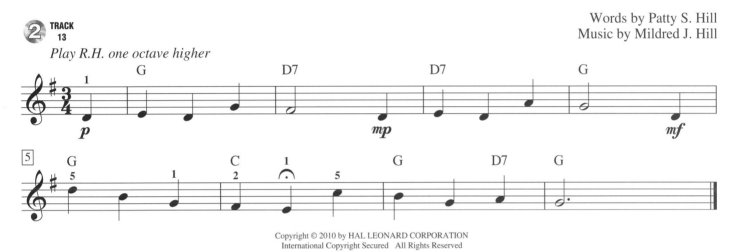

Creating a V7 Introduction

You can create an easy introduction to "Good Morning to All" by playing a V7 (dominant 7th) arpeggio in the key of the piece. You can find the V7 in any key by locating the fifth note (dominant) in the scale and, using this as the root, build a Major triad plus a seventh.

A V7 chord in any key is made up of the V chord and a 7th.

V7 in G Major is a D7   V7 in G arpeggio

Play "Good Morning to All" using this V7 introduction.
Go back to page 23 and create a V7 introduction to "Alouette" and "For He's a Jolly Good Fellow."

"I Will Remember You" contains shifting meters (time signatures).

1. Write in the counts under the left-hand rhythms.
2. Practice tapping the rhythm while counting aloud.

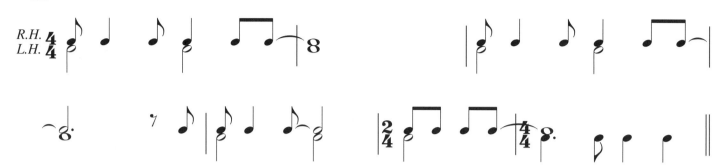

I WILL REMEMBER YOU

Theme from THE BROTHERS McMULLEN

Words and Music by Sarah McLachlan,
Seamus Egan and Dave Merenda
Arranged by Wendy Stevens

Is this piece in C Major or A minor?_____ (Hint: Look at the last measure. Answer on page 96.)

YESTERDAY

Words and Music by John Lennon
and Paul McCartney
Arranged by Wendy Stevens

Unit 5

Triplets

A **triplet** divides the beat into three equal parts. Be careful to make the three subdivisions equal to each other.

Clap and count aloud.

1. Finish writing in the counts under the left-hand rhythms.
2. Practice tapping the rhythm while counting aloud.

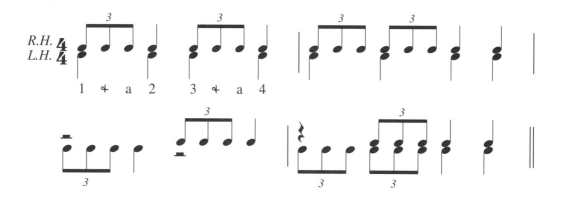

Practice these exercises singing the words, then singing the counts.

The italicized 3 indicates a triplet, not a finger number.

72

Tap and count the "Marche Slav" rhythm pattern. Be careful to keep the triplet rhythm even.

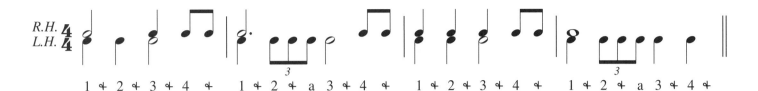

mf–f Play *mezzo forte* the first time.
Play *forte* on the repeat.

MARCHE SLAV
(Slavonic March, Op. 31)

By Pyotr Il'yich Tchaikovsky (1840–1893)
Arranged by Wendy Stevens

TRACKS 19/20

Boldly (♩ = 100)
(2nd time R.H. 8va)

F Major Scale

 Circle the Bs that are made flat by this key signature.

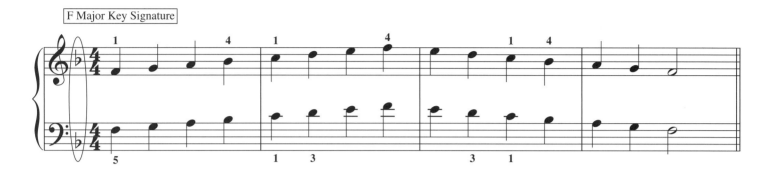

Primary Chords in Root Position

Primary chords are built on the 1st, 4th, and 5th notes in a scale, thus the I, IV, V designation. The V7 chord adds an interval of a 7th above the root.

Chord Progression

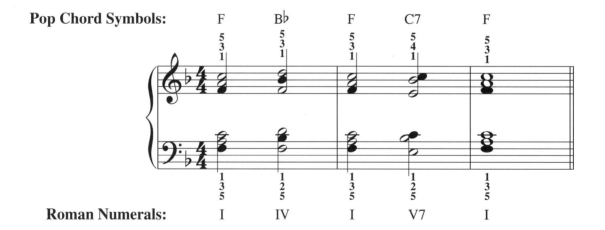

Arpeggio

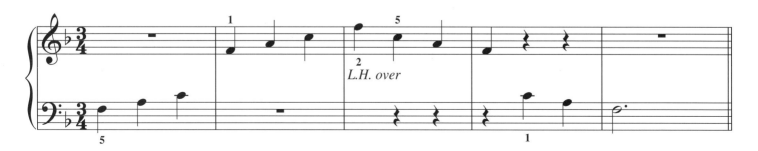

74

AMAZING GRACE

Words by John Newton
Traditional American Melody
Arranged by Wendy Stevens

Duet Playing

Tap and count this rhythm found in the secondo part of "Stand by Me."

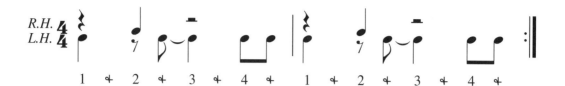

STAND BY ME

Secondo

Words and Music by Jerry Leiber,
Mike Stoller and Ben E. King
Arranged by Wendy Stevens

Making music with other pianists is a very rewarding experience. When practicing duet music, give careful attention to the following:

- **Rhythm –** careful counting will ensure that you are able to play rhythmically with your duet partner.
- **Dynamics –** usually only one player has the melody at a time. Though not always notated, this melody should be played slightly louder than the other part.
- **Listening –** playing together requires you to not only focus on your part, but also listen to and stay together with your partner. Listen to, and become familiar with your partner's music before attempting to play together.

STAND BY ME

Primo

Words and Music by Jerry Leiber,
Mike Stoller and Ben E. King
Arranged by Wendy Stevens

79

Con fuoco – with fire

FINALE

(from *Symphony No. 9*)

By Antonin Dvořák (1841–1904)
Arranged by Wendy Stevens

Playing from Lead Sheets

Lavender's Blue

Harmonize this melody by adding left-hand blocked chords.

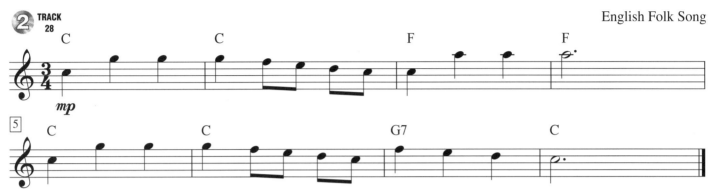

English Folk Song

Broken chords

Playing broken chords in the left hand will create more rhythmic interest.

Pattern A
This pattern is a literal broken chord.

Pattern B
This pattern uses the root, the 5th, and the root of the chord an octave higher.
This pattern may be used to create more depth and space in the sound.

Play "Lavender's Blue" harmonizing it with pattern A and pattern B.

Twinkle, Twinkle, Little Star

Harmonize this tune with broken chords.

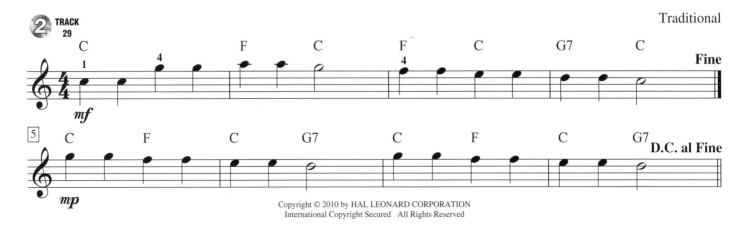

Traditional

Practice the opening measures of "What a Wonderful World" by blocking the left-hand broken chords.

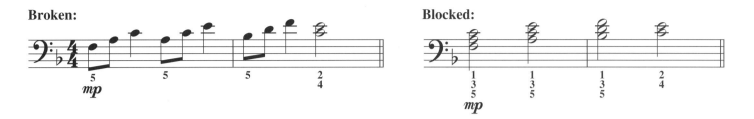

WHAT A WONDERFUL WORLD

Words and Music by George David Weiss
and Bob Thiele
Arranged by Wendy Stevens

world."

The col - ors of the rain - bow, so

pret - ty in the sky, are al - so on the fac - es of

peo - ple go - in' by. I see friends shak - in' hands, say - in', "How do you do?"

mf

They're real - ly say - in', "I love you." I hear ba - bies cry, ___ I

mp

watch them grow; _ they'll learn much more than I'll ev - er know, and I

think to my - self, "What a won - der - ful world."

Yes, I think to my - self, ___ "What a won - der - ful

p

world."

rit.

YOU RAISE ME UP

Words and Music by Brendan Graham
and Rolf Lovland
Arranged by Wendy Stevens

Unit 6

New Time Signature

$\frac{3}{8}$ Three eighth notes fill one measure.
♪ = 1 beat.

 Remember that the eighth note ♪ equals 1 beat.
Fill in the blanks with the correct number of beats.

♪ = ___   ♩ = ___   ♩. = ___

Clap and count aloud.

1. Write in the counts to this rhythm.
2. Practice clapping or tapping the rhythm while counting aloud.

SCARBOROUGH FAIR

Traditional English
Arranged by Wendy Stevens

TRACKS 34/35

Calmly (♪ = 132)

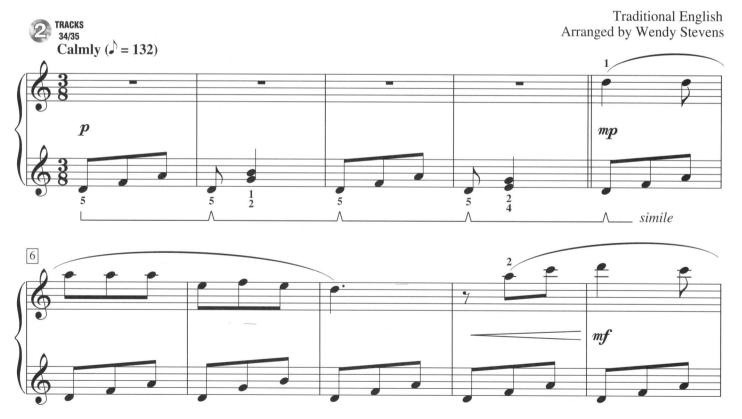

Answers on page 96

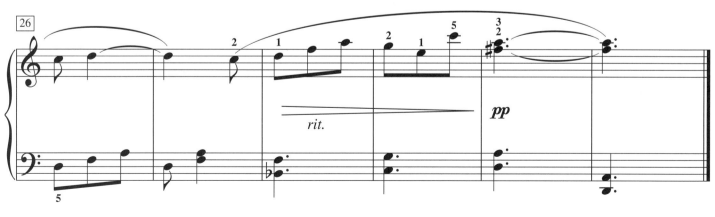

New Time Signature

Clap and count aloud.

1. Write in the counts under the left-hand rhythms.
2. Practice tapping the rhythm while counting aloud.

MEMORY
from CATS

Music by Andrew Lloyd Webber
Text by Trevor Nunn after T.S. Eliot
Arranged by Wendy Stevens

Mid - night. _____ Not a sound from the
Mem - ory _____ all a - lone in the

pave - ment. _____ Has the moon lost her mem - ory? _____ She is smil - ing a -
moon - light _____ I can smile at the old days, _____ I was beau - ti - ful

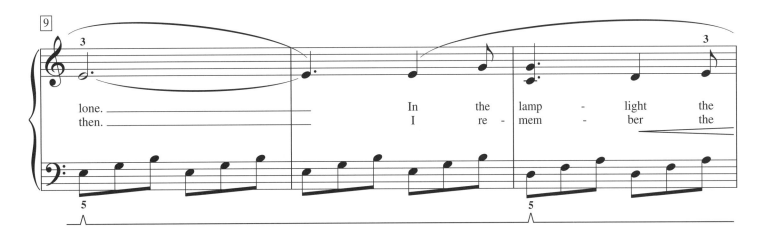

Practice this syncopated exercise to prepare for "The Music of the Night."

THE MUSIC OF THE NIGHT
from THE PHANTOM OF THE OPERA

Music by Andrew Lloyd Webber
Lyrics by Charles Hart
Additional Lyrics by Richard Stilgoe
Arranged by Wendy Stevens

1. Label the chords below as I or V7.
2. Practice this left-hand exercise to prepare for "Hungarian Rhapsody No. 2."

> ***Accelerando*** means to gradually increase the tempo of the piece.

HUNGARIAN RHAPSODY NO. 2

By Franz Liszt (1811–1886)
Arranged by Wendy Stevens

TRACKS
40/41

Begin slowly, gradually increasing speed

Answers on page 96

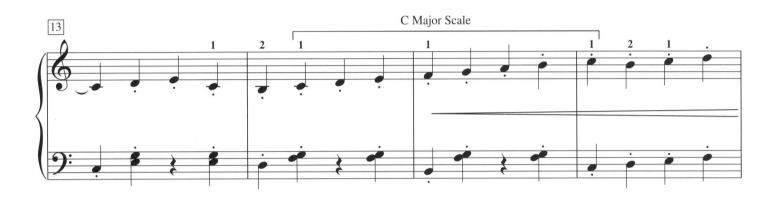

Answer Key

Page 7

Line 1: F, C, D, G, C

Line 2: F, B, G, C, E

Page 8

Line 1: 4th, 2nd, 3rd, 8th, 5th, 7th

Line 2: 5th, 2nd, 7th, 4th, 3rd, 6th

Page 18

Line 1: 2nd, 3rd, 4th, 5th

Line 2: 2nd, 3rd, 4th, 5th

Line 4: 2nd, 3rd, 4th, 5th, 3rd, 7th, 3rd, 8th

Page 33

The syncopation in "Turkey in the Straw" occurs in measures 7, 9, 10, 11, 12 and 15 when the quarter note lands on the "and" of beat one.

Page 51

E Minor, D Minor, B Minor, A Minor

Page 52

C Major

Page 56

F Major

Page 61

G Major

Page 69

C Major

Page 88

Eighth note = 1, Quarter note = 2, Dotted quarter note = 3

Page 93

V7, I